Following in His Footsteps

The Blessings of Living Out Our Faith

Playing hide-and-seek is a fun game! But we
should never hide our love for Jesus!

Jesus said, "You are the light of the World. You don't light a candle and hide it but you place it where it lights up the whole house."
(Matthew 5:15)

When Jesus was on earth, people could see God in Him by the good things He did for others.

Which person is letting their light shine?
Draw rays of light around their circle!

Jesus told a story about a shepherd who separated the sheep from the goats. The sheep did what the shepherd asked them. The goats did not.

Following Jesus means following
in His footsteps!

Swimming in the ocean doesn't
make us a fish.

In the same way, sitting in a church doesn't make us a Christian. We are Christians, when we follow God's ways.

The wise builder built his house on a rock
and it stood strong! When we do what God tells us,
we are wise!

The foolish builder built his house
on the sand. When the storms came, it fell.
When we don't do what God tells us, we are foolish!

Doing the right thing is not always easy.
But doing the right thing is always
the right thing to do.

Just like anything you want to become good at, being a good follower of Jesus takes effort and practice.

Help Clarissa get to the place where she can
let her light shine.

God is happy when we obey him and we treat
others with great kindness and respect.
Remember, what we do to others
we are doing to Him.

Jesus said, "In this way people will know that you are My followers, by the love you have for each other."